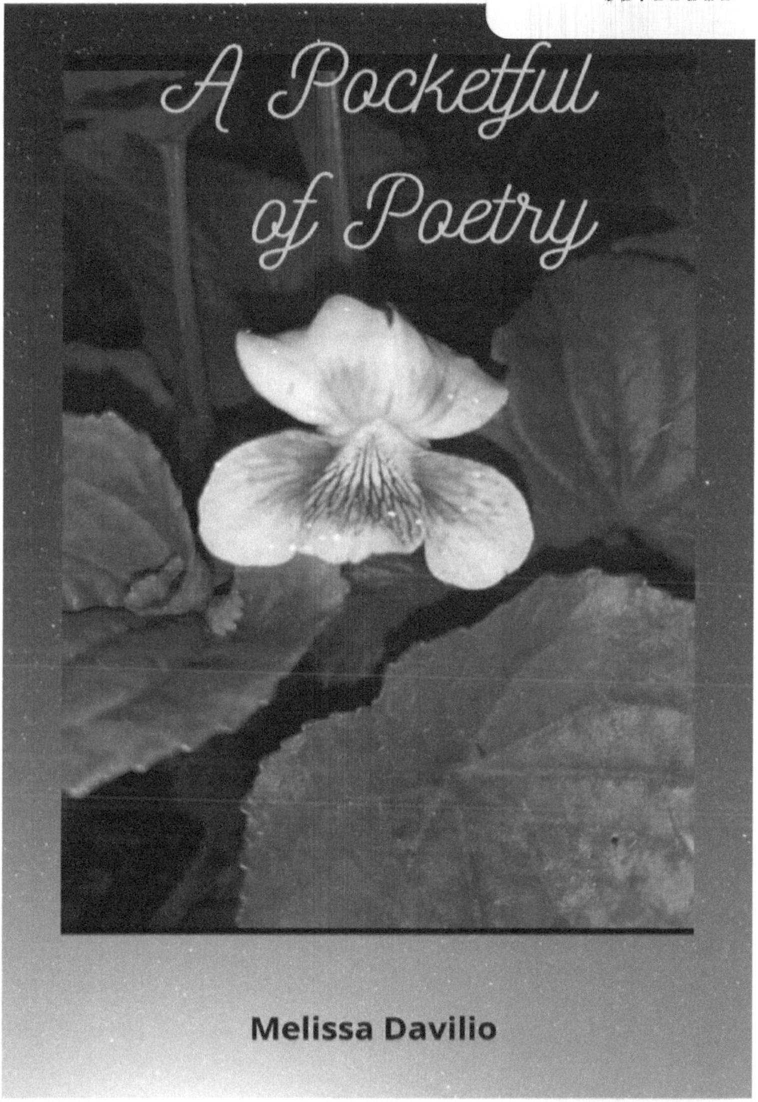

A Pocketful of Poetry

Melissa Davilio

Table of Contents

In a Warm Summer Glade
(Abhanga)

a butterfly flutters
in a field painted jade
in a warm Summer Glade -
savored moments

Alabaster Swan
(Acrosteleostic)

Summer sunshine shifts to flakes of snow
Under gray clouds hinting at ennui
Masquerading as an alabaster swan
Mounded upon a statue of cement
Euphoric cherub with wings spread wide
Reveling in the beauty of winter

Hibiscus (Acrostic)

Hibiscus blossoms painted
In pink palladium
Blooming petals bursting with color
Innocent as children
Slices of simplicity
Crowning a flower garden
Umbrellas raised to capture
Silver slivers of Summer rain

But for the Roses
(Adonics Poetry)

But for the roses
I'd think you were here
Silence was our norm
Something that I hear
More now that you're gone

Kaleidoscope (Alouette)

Butterflies flutter
seeming to stutter
through a field of pink pansies
tiptoeing their dance
a hop, skip and prance
kaleidoscope of gypsies

Frittering away
a hot Summer day
skittering above the grass
as the sun sinks low
upon the meadow
where they disappear en masse

Ladybug (American 767)

lovely little ladybug
without reservation
clings to my outstretched finger

Water and Earth (Antonym Diamante)

water
crisp, clean
dripping, dropping, flowing
dewdrops, rivers / rust, dirt
corroding, eroding, blowing
dusty, musty
earth

Come Dawn (Aubade)

Must we awaken with the roses
as the sun so early rises?
Must I miss the beating of your heart
when we once again this morning part?

Snowflakes (Badger's Hexastich)

snowflakes
fall in flurries
with dainty elegance
twinkling tufts of tinsel
tiny crystal
monsoon

Go in Peace (Benison)

May your guardian angel
watch over your beautiful face
and bestow her loving grace
upon you.
May you go in peace.

Black Widow
(Bergerette)

dark attic windows
when the wind billows
creaking
face of a widow
within the shadows
peeking
out of the gallows
into the shallows
seeking

Storm Cloud Brooding (Blunden)

beside a river in the woods
within a field abloom
in an elegant pink cascade
perfection on display
while in the sky a storm cloud broods
hints at impending doom

Snow Storm (Boketto)

delicate snowflakes twinkle
as they tumble to the earth
blanketing it in silence
belaboring my sorrow
amid my wonder

its beauty is enthralling
my memories are calling
to my heart

Honeysuckle (Bon-Bon)

honeysuckle
blossoms into
delicate

blooms exploding
with a silent
boom

The Wind Whispers
(Bon-Bon)

the wind whispers
wispy words
in which I hear

but an echo,
my heart beating
with the universe

Azure Sky (Breccbairdne)

Azure sky painted
tangerine in measure
lavender and coral
treasure in the azure

Crickets (Brevette)

crickets
chirping
silence

Flowers (Brevette)

flowers
bursting
blooms

Alabaster Sand
(Bussokuseki)

alabaster sand
shifting upon the shoreline
sifting through clear glass
encapsulated moments
here and past

Blossoms Bursting Blue (Byr A Thoddaid)

Quiet desperation settles
over a field filled with nettles
Bumblebees buzz in the petals blooming
from blossoms bursting blue

Gypsy Butterfly (Cadae)

beautiful
soul
blue butterfly
wise
old crone gypsy queen
rejuvenated with her rebirth
the earth
rejoices in her presence
within her essence
her silence
commands reverence
flittering within a lavender field
dancing with the delicate daisies
as the ruler of her realm

The Gray (Cameo)

The time
never stops, tick tocks
through the end of every day,
as the sun sinks into the
horizon,
and the darkness begins to fall,
washing me away into
the gray.

Vines (Cantar)

Delicate tendrils of ivy,
up the trunk of an oak tree climb,
twining towards its tall branches -
a spider web woven from vines.

Moon Dance
(Casbairdne)

In silence, in the dark night,
in their passion the stars dance,
prancing within the moonlight,
a sight that inspires, enchants.

White Lotus Blossom (Chann)

white lotus blossom
an iridescent jewel
of incandescence

Cardinal (Chi' Yen Shih)

a cardinal sweetly sings
beneath an indigo sky
twittering upon the breeze
while on scarlet wings he flies

As Winter Approaches (Chinese Literary Form)

As Winter approaches, and frost coats the
barren ground,
The last of the leaves tumble to their
demise.
I visit the site of your grave.
Canadian geese wave their goodbye with
a flap of their unfurled wings.

Dragonfly (Chinese Literary Form)

A dragonfly hunts in an amethyst field
Scavenging for its unwary prey
He lures me in with his flattering words
How many victims have fallen today?

Foxglove Petals (Cinqku)

salmon
and yellow
foxglove petals
pink painted lips posing
mid-pout

Lilac Bouquet (Cinquain)

Lilac
blossoms blooming
into soft perfection
delicate floral arrangement
Bouquet

Snow Storm (Cinquain)

Sundry
crystals tumble
blanket the tender grass
enshroud the trees with their caress
Snow storm

A White Orchid (Collum Lune)

a white orchid
growing in an emerald glade
silk blossoms bloom

Early Spring (Cyhedd Hir)

the singing of birds, pink cherry blossoms,
days growing longer, butterfly wings,

blooming daffodils, a warmth to the
breeze, tumbling rain showers, early
Spring

The Tumult of the Ocean (Cyrch A Chwta)

The tumult of the ocean
is like a healing potion
with natural compulsion
creating a commotion
evoking deep emotion
with its rhythm and motion
the explusion of the waves
inspiring great devotion

Pigeons (Cywdd Deuair Fyrion)

pigeons preening
feathers cleaning

perched on stoops
free from their coops

August Sunset (Cywdd Llosgyrnog)

Gazing at an August sunset
remembering the day we met
as I fret about the clouds
billowing in the summer breeze
silhouettes cast upon the trees
wrapping me in silence loud

In the Dead of Winter
(Death Poem)

Now in the dead of Winter
she has become a fragile thing

No longer a delicate flower
blooming in early Spring

Nor is she the beautiful
bountiful Harvest Queen

Her crimson petals
have faded into cinnamon

Wind Song (Decastich)

a whisper in the trees
a rustling of the leaves
sometimes blustery
sometimes a breeze
a susurrated moment
suspended, floating
capable of compassion
yet able to chill the night air
tussling, tumbling, troubling
carrier of pigeons and change

Into the Universe (Dionel)

The moment I expel my final breath
I'll be expelled into the universe
becoming at one with infinity
infiltrating the primordial mist
amazed by the beauty of the abyss
embracing me in its divinity
Into the silence I will be dispersed
within the obsidian upon my death
into the universe

Constellations (Dizain)

constellations filled with flickering stars
shifting, alternating realities,
drifting closer then migrating afar,
almost as fickle as a Summer breeze,
shimmering, glimmering, glistening seas
of diamonds floating through the
universe,
in a dance choreographed and rehearsed,
upon a stage of obsidian, black,
to them desperate people pray and curse,
while they just stoically stare back

And in the Gloaming (Doha)

And in the gloaming, at the coming of the night,
a moth flutters its wings, attracted to twilight

The Whisper of the Whippoorwill (Doha)

A whippoorwill whispers on a summer evening,
weaving the obsidian into winding spells.

Spring (Double Tectractys)

the
balm of
lilac blooms
Spring's arrival
cherry blossoms budding, bursting soon
daffodils, crocuses and witch hazel
filling the air
with their spiced
perfume
scent

A Silver Moon (Duodora)

A silver moon,
glistening, listening,
within the darkness,
the obsidian
void of a Fall night,
where the only sound breaking the silence
is the lonely cry of a whippoorwill...

A silver moon,
hints of desperation,
commiserating
with its desolate
crooning, as it keens beneath the
shadows,
hiding just outside my open windowsill.

Tumbling Autumn Leaves
(Englyn Cyrch)

Tumbling Autumn leaves express
the coming Winter's darkness
leading me into the gray
to the fray without duress.

Ocean Scene (Etheree)

White
seashells
thrash, while waves
crash sand lined shores,
seagulls soar like sailboats
above foam flecked blue water,
dolphins, darting, dip among
roiling, brine filled divets, gray fins
disappearing within the darker depths,
expelling plumes of breath when they
emerge

A Rose Among the Thorns (Free Verse)

Her endurance
comes from within,
allowing her to shine
in times of strife,
resiliency which
now blooms
to life,
a rose among
the thorns

Before the Storm (Free Verse)

Before the rain, our lives weren't divided.
We existed in unison, ebbing and flowing
with the tide. Beach and ocean wrapped
in the warm rays of the sun,
Oblivious to the building thunderclouds,
the current strengthening to an
undertow, a violin's crescendo,
Silent, violent, poignant
Discord
So deafening it drowned us
With its torrential downpour.

Blessed Be (Free Verse)

All hail Mother Earth -
the soil beneath our feet,
the air that we breathe,
the water that keeps us alive,
the flame that keeps us warm,
the forests and the trees,
the butterflies,
the bumblebees,
the rain that falls in torrents,
for without her we cannot survive.

All hail Mother Earth,
and her daily sacrifice,
her infinity,
her divinity,
her femininity,
our paradise.
Blessed be.

Blue Butterflies (Free Verse)

An azure swarm in a wooded thicket,
Worshippers paying homage to their
queen
A florescent kaleidoscope

Crystal gypsies with translucent wings,
Fluttering with ethereal ease,
But a whisper in the mossy sea,
A mystical vision
on the horizon
at dusk

Clarissa (Free Verse)

She was an island
Unto herself
Isolated
In a cyan sea
Content
In just being alone.

Her thoughts
Like golden leaves
Rustling
In the breeze
Of her brilliant smile.

Flower Child (Free Verse)

flower child
born among the blades of grass
dancing in the breeze
barefoot on a path of strewn pebbles
you are a rebel
a daredevil
moving with a flowing, graceful ease
dallying with the sassafras
wild flower

Lavender Bouquet (Free Verse)

Her voice was like a lullaby,
melodious,
soothing and serene,
gentle like a Summer breeze,
as calming as a cerulean pool
on a languid afternoon,
lovely like a lavender bouquet,
on display,
in a field painted jade

'Neath the Shadowed Boughs (Free Verse)

Each sunrise rendered her breathless
Brushing her cheek with a gentle caress
Every morning a reason to live

Engulfed in its tender embrace
Suspended in the ethereal space
'Neath the shadowed boughs

Her reverie undisturbed
By the fluttering of a songbird
Flying on wings of joy

Ocean Song (Free Verse)

Ocean waves thrashing,
Crashing
Explosions
Against the
Nearby rocks.

Seashells sinking as the water washes
Over them -
Never-ending,
Graceful song.

Past Bloom (Free Verse)

Even as the rose petals were spread,
shed like crimson tears,
I felt as if I was still in full bloom,
even as my blossoms were tossed in
mourning,
fluttering to rest within the dirt,
as if floating with the tide,
drifting in the briny sea

Winter Queen (Free Verse)

Lovely maiden bedecked in white,
with skirts that billow in the breeze,
arms outstretched to embrace the night,
whispering among the trees,
dancing in the midnight air,
like a vision or a dream,
eyes that twinkle with a knowing gleam,
spreading yuletide cheer,
humble maiden,
devoted mother,
royal winter queen

Wisdom Whispering
(Free Verse)

Wisdom whispers from the wings
of an owl in flight,
Whisking through the mountain winds,
with its prey in sight
Talons outstretched to grasp
A voracious mind
in its clasp

Mountain by the Sea
(Gammo Haneka)

Beside the ocean, lining the coast
stands a gentle giant ghost.
Its peak is hidden by the mist.

To many creatures it plays host.
Moss laden paths and trails it boasts.
To be discovered they insist.

Its features I enjoy the most
when navigated right up close.
Perfect spot for nature tryst.

In the Soft White Sands
(Glawn)

shifting tourmaline ocean
shimmering in the bright sun
seashells glimmer in motion
in the soft white sands are spun
inspiring a devotion
by the shallow waves are stung
susurrated commotion
a lullaby sweetly sung

Seagulls (Gogyonka)

Seagulls surf
the wind's waves
upon sails
stitched from feathers
to survive the swales.

Cherry Blossoms (Golda)

cherry
blossoms
in full bloom,
pink
puffs of perfumed
fragrance
capture
me
with their
poignant punches,
reminiscent
moments

A Sea of Peonies
(Grayette)

a sea
of peonies
among the jade and sassafras
with petals ruffling in the breeze
delicate blades
of grass
chartreuse
in the sunlight
are blowing in slow motion
vanilla lace a dazzling white
a verdant lush
ocean

A Robin Chirping (Haiku)

a robin chirping
to greet the rising sun
spritz of morning dew

Cherry Blossoms (Haiku)

cherry blossoms
fuchsia florets bursting
into elegance

Sugar Magnolia (Haiku)

sugar magnolia
magenta blossoms
into flowers

Tiger Lilies (Haikuette)

petals of pure silk
a tawny tangerine
saffron pollen flecks

The Night (Jagarti)

The night inspires devotion
silence whispering.

As a Rose Petal Fades
(Jisei)

As a rose petal
fades, garnet into salmon,
losing its luster,
so, too, does its fragrance wane.

Coral Covered Trees
(Kelly Lune)

sun rising over
canopies
coral covered trees

Four Seasons (Kerf)

mahogany petals
on an early March morning
blossoms blooming upon branches once
bare

in the rambling nettles
mass of mosquitoes swarming
in early June when the weather is fair

tattooed tips of oak leaves
tiny specks of September
tinted tangerine by the cool night air

icicles hung on eaves
frozen hints of December
'neath a full moon in a sky crystal clear

Azure Skyline (Kimo)

azure skyline painted in tangerine
transforming the horizon
upon the sun's demise

A Field of Daisies (Kural)

Butterflies fill a field
replete with daisies.

Tulips in a Field (Lady's Slipper)

A field of tulips wield
soft petals juxtaposed
in curling swirls of red

At Dawn (Luc Bat)

the chillier weather
the smell of a leather jacket
stark oak tree silhouettes
and twirling pirouettes of leaves
fluttering in the breeze
the distant memories of you
'neath a sky baby blue
my heart breaking in two at dawn

Come Dawn (Luc Bat)

early Spring morning scene,
field painted tangerine, green grass
loaded with sassafras
rejuvenating fast in May,
bluebirds chatter away
at the start of the day, come dawn

Heather (Mesostich)

a landscape, plush, filled with downy
grass, painted green - purple mottled
buds lifted to praise the rising sun,
pleasantly greeting a waving daisy -
leaving me breathless, as I collapse
beneath the raised umbrella of pale
clouds, tinted coral in celebration

p

Ants in the Grass (Mirror Poem)

Ants in the grass,
en masse enchant
mobbing the scene
green grassy globs
prancing the ground
bounding they dance
sun shimmering
glimmer as one

A Songbird Sits
(Octastich)

A songbird sits
among the blossoms
of a tree in bloom

Its cheerful song
drifts upon the breeze
at the first hint of dawn
on a Spring morning
amidst the drops of dew

Into the Ether (Octastich)

And upon my death
I shall journey into the ether,
where time ceases to exist,
where nobody insists,
I be anything but myself,
where a wealth of mystery unfolds,
and I am free to behold
its infinite beauty.

The Here and Now
(Octastich)

The sun washes away the creases
from a troubled brow,
easing the pain of waking,
creeping over the horizon,
shedding dawn upon the lake,
as gentle rocks silently,
violently break the surface,
and I inhale the here and now.

A Primrose Petal
(Oriental Octet)

a primrose petal
perched upon its perky stem
reaches for the sky
stretching to collect the dew
dainty, delicate, exquisite
perfection pictured
in the shimmer of the sun
enchanting maiden

Waves (Paeon)

Mesmerizing
    ululations,
oceanic
    susurrations,
undulations
    of resplendent
        independence

Constellation (Quatrain)

The stars ameliorated my pain
as I drifted, fading away
into the comforting confines
of their constellation

The Wings of Butterflies (Quintain)

What if the wings of butterflies
are the skeletons of broken dreams
recycled by the universe,
tattered tendrils woven into lace,
painted with a precision unrehearsed

Tiny Tinsel Shavings
(Quintain)

myriad stars
illuminating the night
like tiny tinsel shavings
shimmering, shining bright
sparkling crystal lights

Snowfallen (Rhyme)

Silver kisses
gossamer wishes
iridescent diamonds dancing
delightfully entrancing
beneath the moonlight
twinkling like starlight
descending in the dark
like silent remarks
blanketing the trees
covering the leaves
shimmering in the night

Twilight (Scallop)

twilight
the dawn of dusk
a stillness in the air
and the moon's vacant stare
as the stars blush
come night

A Sparrow (Sedoka)

a sparrow
sweetly sings
on a summer morning

its gentle melody
recalls in me
once sung lullabies

Gypsy Wildflower
(Sedoka)

gypsy wildflower
gently blowing in the breeze
on a summer afternoon

traipsing through the grass
barefoot on a pebble path
I long to be just like you

Sparrow (Sedoka)

Sparrow perched upon thin branch
wings outspread
singing to the sun

Lovely lullaby
once I sung
while I rocked your cradle

Daffodils in an Emerald Glade (Sesain)

Yellow bonnets on nodding heads
in a field painted jade
Gypsies dancing barefoot
among the waist-high grass
wearing carnelian masks
Daffodils in an emerald glade

Nectarine Moonlight
(Sesain)

The stars twinkle in tangerine
reflect in a pool of aquamarine
set in a field of velvet green
while the moon rises
a nectarine
illuminating the sky

Tectonic Plates (Sesain)

Tectonic plates
shift beneath the surface
before the volcano explodes
releasing ash
and the lava flows
coursing down my nose

A Black Widow's Web (Seven-Eleven Couplet Rhyme)

woven whispers echo, ebb
between the tendrils of a black widow's
web

The Fragrance (Somonka)

the fragrance
of a red rose bouquet
pales in comparison
to your perfume
scented kiss

even the dove
misses the sparrow
in the winter
waiting for the bliss
of the coming spring

The Night Sky
(Spondiddle)

whispers the wind as it blows in the night
subtle the moon with its soft silver light
the stars all a shimmer
with glistening grace
the sky is a glimmer
a beautiful place

A Delicate Rose (Tan Renga)

a delicate rose
her perfume wafts
across the room

garnet flowers delivered
in a crystal vase exposed

A Dainty Daisy (Tanka)

a dainty daisy
delicate petals extending
into the wide open spaces
of an empty field
as Spring arrives

A Monarch Butterfly (Tanka)

a monarch butterfly
flutters throughout
a meadow
rife with verdant
tulip blossoms in bloom

A Robin Chirps (Tanka)

a robin chirps
its cheerful song
as if just for me
and my melancholy
is gone

A Soft Wind Blows
(Tanka)

a soft wind blows
through the trees
billowing leaves
dangle in the air
like exhaled breaths

Caterpillars (Tanka)

caterpillars
creep into
their cozy wombs
cocoons that resemble
cryptic tombs

Coral Kasumi Blooms
(Tanka)

coral kasumi blooms
lined with pink and puce
delicate, fragile, frail
newborn baby inhales
first exquisite breath

Pink Cherry Blossoms
(Tanka)

pink cherry blossoms
dangling above my forehead
sweet scent of flowers
potent puffs of her perfume
captivating my senses

Plumes of Breath (Tanka)

Plumes of breath
infiltrating the night air
as snowflakes tumble
with a hint of resignation
knowing they'll soon disappear

Thorns Expose (Tanka)

thorns expose
the beauty of a rose
reposing
within the comfort
of the rain

Timid Titmouse (Tanka)

Timid titmouse
cowering in the shadows,
why do you hide from me?
What is that you fear?
Could it be my reprisal?

Tranquil Waves (Tanka)

tranquil waves
cascading a rocky shore
flecks of frothy foam
reminiscent of the tears
I wept upon your grave

Weep Not in Sorrow
(Tanka)

weep not in sorrow
for even snowflakes
cease to glisten
before seeping into the soil
at the onset of spring

An Orange Butterfly (Tanka/Haiku)

an orange butterfly
rests its wings
upon a blade of grass
as delicate as the breath
of a newborn baby

the monarch flutters
in a green field -
an infant's tiny gasps

A Robin's Song (Taylor)

Upon striated wings
a robin flies
the song it sings
resounding in an azure sky
on high

Sunrise (Tetractys)

sun
rising
in the sky
breathing to life
the stark silhouette of the horizon

Sunset (Tetractys)

sun
setting
in the sea
in tangerine
explosion on a sultry horizon

Honeybee (Toddaid Hir)

Honeybee asleep in its hive - dreaming
of blossoms livestreaming,
slumbers like an innocent child - lost
hours
among the wild flowers

Willow in the Wilderness
(Triolet)

a willow in the wilderness
wearing a woven gown
wanton maiden, crone, goddess
a willow in the wilderness
in her embrace I coalesce
bow before her wooden crown
a willow in the wilderness
wearing a woven gown

Collecting Seashells
(Trochadiddle)

collecting seashells by light of the moon
my footprints sinking into the sand dunes
tiptoe in the shallows
whisper of the sea
within the dark shadows
so delicately

Gray Boulders (Vakh)

tumultuous waves thrashing,
cascading over gray boulders,
inundating, smashing, crashing,
upon the silent sentries' shoulders

Soft Tulips Blossom
(Waka)

soft tulips blossom
blooming into perfection
fields painted crimson
decorating the horizon
with the beating of my heart

When the Rain Falls (Wheelbarrow)

when the rain
falls
I am enthralled
by
its welcome presence
sinking
into its simple
essence

Poison Hemlocks (Wu Yan)

hemlocks blooming in the Spring
blossom into delicate vanilla clusters
bursting blasts of white poison
with venomous words vicious attacks
without an ounce of decency
spun within their woven lace
as they spew their vitriol
disgraces to the human race

The Break of Dawn (Ya Du)

the break of dawn
the snow gone fast
at last it's Spring -
the rising sun
indicates Winter is done

Hasu (Zappai)

Pale blue transcendence
Hasu's simple devotion
Blooms with purity

Metamorphosis (Ziket)

chrysalis emerging anew
metamorphosis

Two Pigeons (Ziket)

two perching pigeons pirouette
on a church rafter

About the Author

Melissa Davilio is a domestic violence and narcissistic abuse survivor and awareness advocate. She resides in Bristol, CT with her husband, James Hart, and their furry children. She writes nature-based poetry to promote recovery and healing.

www.floatingdownthedelaware.com